Air Fryer Oven Cookbook for Beginners 2021

Amazingly Easy Recipes to Fry, Bake, Grill, and Roast with Your Instant Vortex Air Fryer Oven

Jessica Harris

Table of Contents

Introduction

The multi-functional Instant Vortex Air Fryer is made to start your adventure in cooking. To do so successfully, though, you must start learning all the functions and options that this great kitchen helper has. Yes, it is exciting, and we all want to rush off and start cooking and baking, which is excellent. Staring at the results of flopped recipes is not so great, though. See what you may need to buy extra and take to heart the tips from people who learned the hard way to do and what not to do.

People often ask why the Instant Vortex Air Fryer Oven has so many different cooking modes when the different modes are the same. The reason for this is that the Vortex uses smart programming to assist you in air frying, baking, etcetera at the optimal temperatures and best pre-selected times. The programming is intuitive and guides you along through the whole cooking process. It tells you when to add the food, when to rotate the cooking trays, and when to remove it. What makes the Vortex different from stovetop cooking and oven baking is that the Vortex uses rapid air circulation to cook and bake food with minimum oil or no oil.

It cooks the foods evenly, both fresh and frozen, with a crisp and crunchy outside while the inside of the food stays moist and soft.

Chapter 1. Breakfast and Brunch

1. Egg, Bacon and Cheese Roll Ups

Preparation Time: 10 minutes

Cooking Time: 25 minutes

Servings: 4

Ingredients:

- 12 slices sugar-free bacon.

- ½ medium green bell pepper; seeded and chopped

- 6 large eggs.

- ¼ cup chopped onion

- 1 cup shredded sharp Cheddar cheese.

- ½ cup mild salsa, for dipping

- 2 tbsp. unsalted butter.

Directions:

1. In a medium skillet over medium heat, melt butter. Add onion and pepper to the skillet and sauté until fragrant and onions are translucent, about 3 minutes.

2. Whisk eggs in a small bowl and pour into skillet. Scramble eggs with onions and peppers until fluffy and fully cooked, about 5 minutes. Remove from heat and set aside.

3. On the work surface, place three slices of bacon side by side, overlapping about ¼-inch. Place ¼ cup scrambled eggs in a heap on the side closest to you and sprinkle ¼ cup cheese on top of the eggs.

4. Tightly roll the bacon around the eggs and secure the seam with a toothpick if necessary. Place each roll into the air fryer basket.

5. Adjust the temperature to 350 Degrees F and set the timer for 15 minutes. Rotate the rolls halfway through the cooking time. Bacon will be brown and crispy when completely cooked. Serve immediately with salsa for dipping.

Nutrition:

Calories: 460

Protein: 28.2g

Fiber: 0.8g

Fat: 31.7g

Carbs: 6.1g

2. Crispy Ham Egg Cups

Preparation Time: 5 minutes

Cooking Time: 12 minutes

Servings: 2

Ingredients:

- 4 large eggs.

- 4: 1-oz. slices deli ham

- ½ cup shredded medium Cheddar cheese.

- ¼ cup diced green bell pepper.

- 2 tbsp. diced red bell pepper.

- 2 tbsp. diced white onion.

- 2 tbsp. full-fat sour cream.

Directions:

1. Place one slice of ham on the bottom of four baking cups.

2. Take a large bowl, whisk eggs with sour cream. Stir in green pepper, red pepper and onion.

3. Pour the egg mixture into ham-lined baking cups. Top with Cheddar. Place cups into the air fryer basket. Adjust the

temperature to 320 Degrees F and set the timer for 12 minutes or until the tops are browned. Serve warm.

Nutrition:

Calories: 382

Protein: 29.4g

Fiber: 1.4g

Fat: 23.6g

Carbs: 6.0g

3. Olives and Kale

Preparation Time: 5 minutes

Cooking Time: 20 minutes

Servings: 4

Ingredients:

- 4 eggs; whisked

- 1 cup kale; chopped.

- ½ cup black olives, pitted and sliced

- 2 tbsp. cheddar; grated

- Cooking spray

- A pinch of salt and black pepper

Directions:

1. Take a bowl, mix the eggs with the rest of the ingredients, except for the cooking spray, and whisk well. Now, take a pan that fits in your air fryer and grease it with the cooking spray, pour the olives mixture inside, spread. Put the pan into the machine and cook at 360°F for 20 minutes. Serve for breakfast hot.

Nutrition: Calories: 220 Fat: 13g Fiber: 4g Carbs: 6g Protein: 12g

4. Stuffed Poblanos

Preparation Time: 10 minutes

Cooking Time: 20 minutes

Servings: 4

Ingredients:

- ½ lb. spicy ground pork breakfast sausage

- 4 large poblano peppers

- 4 large eggs.

- ½ cup full-fat sour cream.

- 4 oz. full-fat cream cheese; softened.

- ¼ cup canned diced tomatoes and green chiles, drained

- 8 tbsp. shredded pepper jack cheese

Directions:

1. In a medium skillet over medium heat, crumble and brown the ground sausage until no pink remains. Remove sausage and drain the fat from the pan. Crack eggs into the pan, scramble, and cook until no longer runny.

2. Place cooked sausage in a large bowl and fold in cream cheese. Mix in diced tomatoes and chiles. Gently fold in eggs.

3. Cut a 4"–5" slit in the top of each poblano, removing the seeds and white membrane with a small knife. Separate the filling into four and spoon carefully into each pepper. Top each with 2 tbsp. pepper jack cheese.

4. Place each pepper into the air fryer basket. Adjust the temperature to 350 Degrees F and set the timer for 15 minutes.

5. Peppers will be soft and cheese will be browned when ready. Serve immediately with sour cream on top.

Nutrition:

Calories: 489

Protein: 22.8g

Fiber: 3.8g

Fat: 35.6g

Carbs: 12.6g

5. Raspberries Oatmeal

Preparation Time: 5 minutes

Cooking Time: 15 minutes

Servings: 4

Ingredients:

- 1 ½ cups coconut; shredded

- ½ cups raspberries

- 2 cups almond milk

- ¼ tsp. nutmeg, ground

- 2 tsp. stevia

- ½ tsp. cinnamon powder

- Cooking spray

Directions:

1. Grease the air fryer's pan with cooking spray, mix all the ingredients inside, cover and cook at 360°F for 15 minutes.

2. Divide into bowls and serve

Nutrition: Calories: 172 Fat: 5g Fiber: 2g Carbs: 4g Protein: 6g

6. Easy Scotch Eggs

Preparation Time: 15 minutes

Cooking Time: 15 minutes

Servings: 4

Ingredients:

- 1-pound ground breakfast sausage

- 3 tablespoons flour

- 4 hard-boiled eggs, peeled

- 1 egg

- 1 tablespoon water

- ¾ cup panko bread crumbs

Directions:

1. In a bowl, mix the sausage and one tablespoon flour.

2. Divide the sausage mixture into four equal parts. Lay one hard-boiled egg in the center, then wrap the sausage around the egg, sealing completely. Repeat with remaining sausage parts and hard-boiled eggs.

3. In a small bowl, whisk the egg and water until smooth.

4. Place the remaining flour and bread crumbs into separate bowls large enough to dredge the sausage-wrapped eggs.

5. Dredge the sausage-wrapped eggs in the flour, then in the whisked egg, and finally coat in the bread crumbs.

6. Arrange them in the basket. Put the air fryer lid on and cook in the preheated air fryer at 375°F for 20 minutes. Flip them over when the lid screen indicates 'TURN FOOD' halfway through or until the sausage is cooked to desired doneness.

7. Remove from the basket and serve on a plate.

Nutrition:

Calories: 509

Total Fat: 16g

Saturated Fat: 5g

Total Carbs: 8g

Net Carbs: 2g

Fiber: 7g

Protein: 24g

Sugar: 16g

Sodium: 785mg

7. Strawberry Toast

Preparation Time: 8 minutes

Cooking Time: 10 minutes

Servings: 4

Ingredients:

- 4 slices bread, ½-inch thick

- 1 cup sliced strawberries

- 1 teaspoon sugar

- Cooking spray

Directions:

1. On a plate, place the bread slices.

2. Arrange the bread slices (sprayed side down) in the air fryer basket. Evenly spread the strawberries onto them and sprinkle them with sugar. Put the air fryer lid on and cook in the preheated air fryer at 375°F for 8 minutes, or until the tops are covered with a beautiful glaze.

3. Remove from the basket and serve on a plate.

Nutrition: Calories: 375 Total Fat: 22g Saturated Fat: 5g Total Carbs: 2g Net Carbs: 2g Fiber: 4g Protein: 14g Sugar: 5g Sodium: 600mg

8. Cinnamon Sweet-Potato Chips

Preparation Time: 7 minutes

Cooking Time: 8 minutes

Servings: 7

Ingredients:

- 1 small sweet potato, cut into 3/8-inch slices

- 2 tablespoons olive oil

- Ground cinnamon

Directions:

1. In a bowl, toss the potato slices in olive oil. Sprinkle with the cinnamon and mix well. Lay the potato slices in the air fryer basket. You may need to work in batches to avoid overcrowding. Put the air fryer lid on and cook in the preheated air fryer at 375°F for 4 minutes. Shake the basket when the lid screen indicates 'TURN FOOD'. Cook for an additional 4 minutes or until fork-tender.

2. Remove from the basket and serve on a large dish lined with paper towels.

Nutrition: Calories: 385 Total Fat: 18g Saturated Fat: 2g Total Carbs: 5g Net Carbs: 3g Fiber: 8g Protein: 20g Sugar: 3g Sodium: 518mg

9. Quiche Muffin Cups

Preparation Time: 11 minutes

Cooking Time: 10 minutes

Servings: 10

Ingredients:

- ¼ pound all-natural ground pork sausage

- Three eggs

- ¾ cup milk

- 4 ounces sharp Cheddar cheese, grated

- One muffin pan

- Cooking spray

Directions:

1. On a clean work surface, slice the pork sausage into 2-ounce portions. Shape each portion into a ball and gently flatten it with your palm.

2. Lay the patties in the air fryer basket and cook in the preheated air fryer at 375°F for 6 minutes. Flip the patties over when the lid screen indicates 'TURN FOOD' during cooking time.

3. Remove the patties from the basket to a large dish lined with paper towels. Crumble them into small pieces with a fork. Set aside.

4. Line a muffin pan with ten paper liners. Lightly spray the muffin cups with cooking spray.

5. Divide crumbled sausage equally among the ten muffin cups and sprinkle the tops with the cheese.

6. Arrange the muffin pan in the air fryer basket.

7. Put the air fryer lid on and cook in the preheated air fryer at 375°F for 8 minutes until the tops are golden and a toothpick inserted in the middle comes out clean.

8. Remove from the basket and let cool for 5 minutes before serving.

Nutrition:

Calories: 497 Total Fat: 25g

Saturated Fat: 2g Total Carbs: 1g

Net Carbs: 1g

Fiber: 4g

Protein: 28g

Sugar: 5g

Sodium: 742mg

Chapter 2. Poultry

10. Cheesy Spinach Stuffed Chicken Breasts

Preparation Time: 20 minutes

Cooking Time: 25 minutes

Servings: 4

Ingredients:

- 1 (10-ounce / 284-g) package frozen spinach, thawed and drained well

- 1 cup feta cheese, crumbled

- 4 boneless chicken breasts

From the Cupboard:

- Salt and ground black pepper to taste

- Special Equipment:

- 4 or 8 toothpicks, soaked for at least 30 minutes

Directions:

1. Preheat the air fryer to 380°F (193°C). Spritz the air fryer basket with cooking spray.

2. Make the filling: Chop the spinach and put it in a large bowl, then add the feta cheese and ½ teaspoon of ground black pepper. Stir to mix well.

3. On a clean work surface, using a knife, cut a 1-inch incision into the thicker side of each chicken breast horizontally. Make a 3-inch long pocket from the incision and keep the sides and bottom intact.

4. Stuff the chicken pockets with the filling and secure with 1 or 2 toothpicks.

5. Arrange the stuffed chicken breasts in the preheated air fryer. Sprinkle with salt and black pepper and spritz with cooking spray. You may need to work in batches to avoid overcrowding.

6. Cook for 12 minutes or until the internal temperature of the chicken reads at least 165°F (74°C). Flip the chicken halfway through the cooking time.

7. Remove the chicken from the air fryer basket. Discard the toothpicks and allow to cool for 10 minutes before slicing to serve.

Nutrition:

Calories: 648

Fat: 38.7g

Carbs: 4.5g Protein: 68.2g

11. Turkey and Pepper Sandwich

Preparation Time: 5 minutes

Cooking Time: 5 minutes

Servings: 1

Ingredients:

- 2 slices whole-grain bread

- 2 teaspoons Dijon mustard

- 2 ounces (57 g) cooked turkey breast, thinly sliced

- 2 slices low-fat Swiss cheese

- 3 strips roasted red bell pepper

From the Cupboard:

- Salt and ground black pepper to taste

Directions:

1. Preheat the air fryer to 330°F (166°C). Spritz the air fryer basket with cooking spray.

2. Assemble the sandwich: On a dish, place a slice of bread, then top the bread with 1 teaspoon of Dijon mustard, use a knife to smear the mustard evenly.

3. Layer the turkey slices, Swiss cheese slices, and red pepper strips on the bread according to your favorite order. Top them with the remaining teaspoon of Dijon mustard and the remaining bread slice.

4. Place the sandwich in the preheated air fryer and spritz with cooking spray. Sprinkle with salt and black pepper.

5. Cook for 5 minutes until the cheese melts and the bread is lightly browned. Flip the sandwich halfway through the cooking time.

6. Serve the sandwich immediately.

Nutrition:

Calories: 328

Fat: 5.0g

Carbs: 38.0g

Protein: 29.0g

12. Spicy Turkey Breast

Preparation Time: 5 minutes

Cooking Time: 40 minutes

Servings: 4

Ingredients:

- 2-pound (907 g) turkey breast

- 2 teaspoons taco seasonings

- 1 teaspoon ground cumin

- 1 teaspoon red pepper flakes

From the Cupboard:

- Salt and ground black pepper to taste

Directions:

1. Preheat the air fryer to 350°F (180°C). Spritz the air fryer basket with cooking spray.

2. On a clean work surface, rub the turkey breast with taco seasoning, ground cumin, red pepper flakes, salt, and black pepper.

3. Arrange the turkey in the preheated air fryer and cook for 40 minutes or until the internal temperature of the turkey reads at

least 165°F (74°C). Flip the turkey breast halfway through the cooking time.

4. Remove the turkey from the basket. Allow cooling for 15 minutes before slicing to serve.

Nutrition:

Calories: 235

Fat: 5.6g

Carbs: 6.6g

Protein: 37.3g

13. Chicken, Mushroom, And Pepper Kabobs

Preparation Time: 1 hour 5 minutes

Cooking Time: 15-20 minutes

Servings: 4

Ingredients:

- ⅓ cup raw honey

- 2 tablespoons sesame seeds

- 2 boneless chicken breasts, cut into cubes

- 6 white mushrooms, cut in halves

- 3 green or red bell peppers, diced

From the Cupboard:

- ⅓ cup soy sauce

- Salt and ground black pepper to taste

- Special Equipment:

- 4 wooden skewers, soaked for at least 30 minutes

Directions:

1. Combine the honey, soy sauce, sesame seeds, salt, and black pepper in a large bowl. Stir to mix well.

2. Dunk the chicken cubes in this bowl, then wrap the bowl in plastic and refrigerate to marinate for at least an hour.

3. Preheat the air fryer to 390°F (199°C). Spritz the air fryer basket with cooking spray.

4. Remove the chicken cubes from the marinade, then run the skewers through the chicken cubes, mushrooms, and bell peppers alternatively.

5. Baste the chicken, mushrooms, and bell peppers with the marinade, then arrange them in the preheated air fryer.

6. Spritz them with cooking spray and cook for 15 to 20 minutes or until the mushrooms and bell peppers are tender and the chicken cubes are well browned. Flip them halfway through the cooking time.

7. Transfer the skewers to a large plate and serve hot.

Nutrition:

Calories: 380

Fat: 16.0g

Carbs: 26.1g

Protein: 34.0g

14. Chicken & Zucchini

Preparation Time: 30 minutes

Cooking Time: 20 minutes

Servings: 6

Ingredients:

- 1/4 cup olive oil

- 1 tablespoon lemon juice

- 2 tablespoons red wine vinegar

- 1 teaspoon oregano

- 1 tablespoon garlic, chopped

- 2 chicken breast fillet, sliced into cubes

- 1 zucchini, sliced

- 1 red onion, sliced

- 1 cup cherry tomatoes, sliced

- Salt and pepper to taste

Directions:

1. In a bowl, mix the olive oil, lemon juice, vinegar, oregano, and garlic.

2. Pour half of the mixture into another bowl.

3. Toss chicken in half of the mixture.

4. Cover and marinate for 15 minutes.

5. Toss the veggies in the remaining mixture.

6. Season both chicken and veggies with salt and pepper.

7. Add chicken to the air fryer basket.

8. Spread veggies on top.

9. Select air fry function. Seal and cook at 380 degrees f for 15 to 20 minutes.

Nutrition:

Calories: 282

Protein: 21.87 g

Fat: 19.04 g

Carbohydrates: 5.31 g

15. Chicken Quesadilla

Preparation Time: 20 minutes

Cooking Time: 30 minutes

Servings: 8

Ingredients:

- 4 tortillas

- Cooking spray

- 1/2 cup sour cream

- 1/2 cup salsa

- Hot sauce

- 12 oz. chicken breast fillet, chopped and grilled

- 3 jalapeño peppers, diced

- 2 cups cheddar cheese, shredded

- Chopped scallions

Directions:

1. Add grill grate to the Ninja Foodi Grill.

2. Close the hood.

3. Choose grill setting.

4. Preheat for 5 minutes.

5. While waiting, spray tortillas with oil.

6. In a bowl, mix sour cream, salsa, and hot sauce. Set aside.

7. Add tortilla to the grate.

8. Grill for 1 minute.

9. Repeat with the other tortillas.

10. Spread the toasted tortilla with the salsa mixture, chicken, jalapeño peppers, cheese, and scallions.

11. Place a tortilla on top. Press.

12. Repeat these steps with the remaining 2 tortillas.

13. Take the grill out of the pot.

14. Choose the roast setting.

15. Cook the Quesadillas at 350F for 25 minutes.

Nutrition:

Calories: 184

Protein: 12.66 g

Fat: 7.66 g

Carbohydrates: 15.87 g

16. Buffalo Chicken Wings

Preparation Time: 15 minutes

Cooking Time: 30 minutes

Servings: 4

Ingredients:

- 2 lb. chicken wings

- 2 tablespoons oil

- 1/2 cup Buffalo sauce

Directions:

1. Coat the chicken wings with oil.

2. Add these to an air fryer basket.

3. Choose air fry function.

4. Cook at 390 degrees F for 15 minutes.

5. Shake and then cook for another 15 minutes.

6. Dip in Buffalo sauce before serving.

Nutrition:

Calories: 376 Protein: 51.93 g

Fat: 16.4 g Carbohydrates: 2.18 g

17. Mustard Chicken

Preparation Time: 20 minutes

Cooking Time: 50 minutes

Servings: 4

Ingredients:

- 1/4 cup Dijon mustard

- 1/4 cup cooking oil

- Salt and pepper to taste

- 2 tablespoons honey

- 1 tablespoon dry oregano

- 2 teaspoons dry Italian seasoning

- 1 tablespoon lemon juice

- 6 chicken pieces

Directions:

1. Combine all the ingredients, except chicken in a bowl.

2. Mix well.

3. Toss the chicken in the mixture.

4. Add a roasting rack to your Ninja Foodi Grill.

5. Choose roast function.

6. Set it to 350 degrees F.

7. Cook for 30 minutes.

Flip and cook for another 15 to 20 minutes.

Nutrition:

Calories: 1781

Protein: 293.44 g

Fat: 54.33 g

Carbohydrates: 11.71 g

Chapter 3. Seafood

18. Bacon-Wrapped Scallops

Preparation Time: 5 minutes

Cooking Time: 10 minutes

Servings: 4

Ingredients:

- 16 sea scallops

- 8 slices bacon, cut in half

- 8 toothpicks

- Salt

- Freshly ground black pepper

Directions:

1. Using a paper towel, pat the dry the scallops.

2. Wrap each scallop with a half slice of bacon. Secure the bacon with a toothpick.

3. Place the scallops into the air fryer in a single layer. (You may need to cook your scallops in more than one batch.)

4. Spray the scallops with olive oil, and season them with salt and pepper.

5. Set the temperature of your Innsky AF to 370°F. Set the timer and fry for 5 minutes.

6. Flip the scallops.

7. Reset your timer and cook the scallops for 5 minutes more.

8. Using tongs, remove the scallops from the air fryer basket. Plate, serve and enjoy.

Nutrition:

Calories: 311

Fat: 17g

Saturated fat: 5g

Carbohydrate: 3g

Fiber: 0g

Sugar: 0g

Protein: 34g

Sodium: 1110mg

19. Indian Almond Crusted Fried Masala Fish

Intermediate Recipe

Preparation Time: 30 minutes

Cooking Time: 20 minutes

Servings: 4

Ingredients:

- 900g of fish fillet

- 4 tablespoons of extra virgin olive oil

- ¾ teaspoon of turmeric

- 1 teaspoon of cayenne pepper

- 1 teaspoon of salt

- 1 tablespoon of fenugreek leaves

- 1 ½ teaspoons of ground cumin

- 2 teaspoons of amchoor powder

- 2 tablespoons of ground almonds

Directions:

1. In a bowl, combine the oil, turmeric, cayenne, salt, fenugreek leaves, and cumin and amchoor powder. After combining the

mix in the ground almonds, put the fish into a bowl and pour the mixture over the fish. Mix around to evenly cover the fish.

2. Put the fish into the Air Fryer basket and cook for 450 degrees Fahrenheit for 10 minutes Turnover and then cook for a further 10 minutes

Nutrition

Calories 675Calories

Fat 43.6g

Carbs 41.7g

Protein 34.5g

20. Air Fryer Salmon

Preparation Time: 5 minutes

Cooking Time: 10 minutes

Servings: 2

Ingredients:

- ½ tsp. salt

- ½ tsp. garlic powder

- ½ tsp. smoked paprika

- Salmon

Directions:

1. Mix spices together and sprinkle onto salmon. Place seasoned salmon into the Air fryer.

2. Close crisping lid. Set temperature to 400°F, and set time to 10 minutes.

Nutrition:

Calories: 185

Fat: 11g;

Protein: 21g Sugar: 0g

21. Lemon Pepper, Butter and Cajun Cod

Preparation Time: 5 minutes

Cooking Time: 12 minutes

Servings: 2

Ingredients:

- 2 (8-ounce) cod fillets, cut to fit into the air fryer basket

- 1 tablespoon Cajun seasoning

- ½ teaspoon lemon pepper

- 1 teaspoon salt

- ½ teaspoon freshly ground black pepper

- 2 tablespoons unsalted butter, melted

- 1 lemon, cut into 4 wedges

Directions:

1. Spray the Innsky air fryer basket with olive oil. Place the fillets on a plate. In a small mixing bowl, combine the Cajun seasoning, lemon pepper, salt, and pepper.

2. Rub the seasoning mix over the fish.

3. Place the cod into the greased air fryer basket. Brush the top of each fillet with melted butter.

4. Set the temperature of your Innsky AF to 360°F. Set the timer and bake for 6 minutes. After 6 minutes, open up your air fryer drawer and flip the fish. Brush the top of each fillet with more melted butter.

5. Reset the timer and bake for 6 minutes more. Squeeze fresh lemon juice over the fillets.

Nutrition:

Calories: 377

Protein: 23.49 g

Fat: 26.1g

Carbohydrates: 11.8 g

22. Steamed Salmon & Sauce

Preparation Time: 5 minutes

Cooking Time: 10 minutes

Servings: 2

Ingredients:

- 1 cup Water

- 2 x 6 oz. Fresh Salmon

- 2 Tsp Vegetable Oil

- A Pinch of Salt for Each Fish

- ½ cup Plain Greek Yogurt

- ½ cup Sour Cream

- 2 tbsp. Finely Chopped Dill (Keep a bit for garnishing)

- A Pinch of Salt to Taste

Directions:

1. Pour the water into the bottom of the fryer and start heating to 285° F.

2. Drizzle oil over the fish and spread it. Salt the fish to taste.

3. Now pop it into the fryer for 10 min.

4. In the meantime, mix the yogurt, cream, dill, and a bit of salt to make the sauce. When the fish is done, serve with the sauce and garnish with sprigs of dill.

Nutrition:

Calories: 223

Protein: 12.12 g

Fat: 16.62 g

Carbohydrates: 7.72 g

23. Salmon Patties

Preparation Time: 5 minutes

Cooking Time: 10 minutes

Servings: 4

Ingredients:

- 1 (14.75-ounce) can wild salmon, drained

- 1 large egg

- ¼ cup diced onion

- ½ cup bread crumbs

- 1 teaspoon dried dill

- ½ teaspoon freshly ground black pepper

- 1 teaspoon salt

- 1 teaspoon Old Bay seasoning

Directions:

1. Spray the Innsky air fryer basket with olive oil. Put the salmon in a medium bowl and remove any bones or skin. Add the egg, onion, bread crumbs, dill, pepper, salt, and Old Bay seasoning and mix well. Form the salmon mixture into 4 equal patties. Place the patties in the greased air fryer basket.

2. Set the temperature of your Innsky AF to 370°F. Set the timer and grill for 5 minutes. Flip the patties. Reset the timer and grill the patties for 5 minutes more. Plate, serve and enjoy.

Nutrition:

Calories: 239;

Fat: 9g

Saturated fat: 2g

Carbohydrate: 11g

Fiber: 1g

Sugar: 1g

Protein: 27g

Iron: 2mg

Sodium: 901mg

24. Sweet and Savory Breaded Shrimp

Preparation Time: 5 minutes

Cooking Time: 20 minutes

Servings: 2

Ingredients:

- ½ pound of fresh shrimp, peeled from their shells and rinsed

- 2 raw eggs

- ½ cup of breadcrumbs (we like Panko, but any brand or home recipe will do)

- ½ white onion, peeled and rinsed and finely chopped

- 1 teaspoon of ginger-garlic paste

- ½ teaspoon of turmeric powder

- ½ teaspoon of red chili powder

- ½ teaspoon of cumin powder

- ½ teaspoon of black pepper powder

- ½ teaspoon of dry mango powder

- Pinch of salt

Directions:

1. Cover the basket of the Air fryer with a lining of tin foil, leaving the edges uncovered to allow air to circulate through the basket.

2. Preheat the Innsky air fryer to 350 degrees. In a large mixing bowl, beat the eggs until fluffy and until the yolks and whites are fully combined. Dunk all the shrimp in the egg mixture, fully submerging. In a separate mixing bowl, combine the bread crumbs with all the dry ingredients until evenly blended. One by one, coat the egg-covered shrimp in the mixed dry ingredients so that fully covered, and place on the foil-lined air-fryer basket.

3. Set the air-fryer timer to 20 minutes. Halfway through the cooking time, shake the handle of the air-fryer so that the breaded shrimp jostles inside and fry-coverage is even. After 20 minutes, when the fryer shuts off, the shrimp will be perfectly cooked and their breaded crust golden-brown and delicious! Using tongs, remove from the air fryer and set on a serving dish to cool.

Nutrition:

Calories: 296

Protein: 35.83 g

Fat: 14.49 g

Carbohydrates: 3.52 g

25. Healthy Fish And Chips

Preparation Time: 5 minutes

Cooking Time: 15 minutes

Servings: 3

Ingredients:

- Old Bay seasoning

- ½ C. panko breadcrumbs

- 1 egg

- 2 tbsp. almond flour

- 4-6-ounce tilapia fillets

- Frozen crinkle cut fries

Directions:

1. Add almond flour to one bowl, beat egg in another bowl, and add panko breadcrumbs to the third bowl, mixed with Old Bay seasoning. Dredge tilapia in flour, then egg, and then breadcrumbs. Place coated fish in the air fryer along with fries.

2. Set temperature to 390°F, and set time to 15 minutes.

Nutrition: Calories: 219 Fat: 5g Protein: 25g Sugar: 1g

26. Indian Fish Fingers

Preparation Time: 35 minutes

Cooking Time: 15 minutes

Servings: 4

Ingredients:

- 1/2pound fish fillet

- 1 tablespoon finely chopped fresh mint leaves or any fresh herbs

- 1/3 cup bread crumbs

- 1 teaspoon ginger garlic paste or ginger and garlic powders

- 1 hot green chili finely chopped

- 1/2 teaspoon paprika

- Generous pinch of black pepper

- Salt to taste

- 3/4 tablespoons lemon juice

- 3/4 teaspoons garam masala powder

- 1/3 teaspoon rosemary

- 1 egg

Directions:

1. Start by removing any skin on the fish, washing, and patting dry. Cut the fish into fingers. In a medium bowl, mix together all ingredients, except for fish, mint, and bread crumbs. Bury the fingers in the mixture and refrigerate for 30 minutes. Remove from the bowl from the fridge and mix in mint leaves. In a separate bowl, beat the egg, pour bread crumbs into a third bowl. Dip the fingers in the egg bowl, then toss them in the bread crumbs bowl.

2. Cook at 360 degrees for 15 minutes, toss the fingers halfway through.

Nutrition:

Calories: 187

Fat: 7g

Protein: 11g

Fiber: 1g

Chapter 4. Vegetables and Sides

27. Baked Yams with Dill

Preparation Time: 10 minutes

Cooking Time: 8 minutes

Servings: 2

Ingredients:

- 2 yams

- 1 tablespoon fresh dill

- 1 teaspoon coconut oil

- ½ teaspoon minced garlic

Directions:

1. Wash the yams carefully and cut them into halves. Sprinkle the yam halves with the coconut oil and then rub with the minced garlic. Place the yams in the air fryer basket and cook for 8 minutes at 400° F. After this, mash the yams gently with a fork and then sprinkle with the fresh dill. Serve the yams immediately.

Nutrition: Calories: 25 Fat: 2.3 g Fiber: 0.2 g Carbs: 1.2 g Protein: 0.4 g

28. Honey Onions

Preparation Time: 10 minutes

Cooking Time: 20 minutes

Servings: 2

Ingredients:

- 2 large white onions

- 1 tablespoon raw honey

- 1 teaspoon water

- 1 tablespoon paprika

Directions:

1. Peel the onions and, using a knife, make cuts in the shape of a cross.

2. Then combine the raw honey and water; stir.

3. Add the paprika and stir the mixture until smooth.

4. Place the onions in the air fryer basket and sprinkle them with the honey mixture.

5. Cook the onions for 16 minutes at 380° F.

6. When the onions are cooked, they should be soft.

7. Transfer the cooked onions to serving plates and serve.

Nutrition:

Calories 102,

Fat 0.6,

Fiber 4.5,

Carbs 24.6,

Protein 2.2

29. Delightful Roasted Garlic Slices

Preparation Time: 10 minutes

Cooking Time: 8 minutes

Servings: 4

Ingredients:

- 1 teaspoon coconut oil

- ½ teaspoon dried cilantro

- ¼ teaspoon cayenne pepper

- 12 ounces garlic cloves, peeled

Directions:

1. Sprinkle the garlic cloves with the cayenne pepper and dried cilantro.

2. Mix the garlic up with the spices, and then transfer to the air fryer basket.

3. Add the coconut oil and cook the garlic for 8 minutes at 400° F, stirring halfway through. When the garlic cloves are done, transfer them to serving plates and serve.

Nutrition: Calories 137, Fat 1.6, Fiber 1.8, Carbs 28.2, Protein 5.4

30. Coconut Oil Artichokes

Preparation Time: 10 minutes

Cooking Time: 13 minutes

Servings: 4

Ingredients:

- 1-pound artichokes

- 1 tablespoon coconut oil

- 1 tablespoon water

- ½ teaspoon minced garlic

- ¼ teaspoon cayenne pepper

Directions:

1. Trim the ends of the artichokes, sprinkle them with the water, and rub them with the minced garlic.

2. Sprinkle with cayenne pepper and coconut oil.

3. After this, wrap the artichokes in foil and place them in the air fryer basket.

4. Cook for 10 minutes at 370° F.

5. Then remove the artichokes from the foil and cook them for 3 minutes more at 400° F.

6. Transfer the cooked artichokes to serving plates and allow to cool a little.

7. Serve.

Nutrition:

Calories 83,

Fat 3.6,

Fiber 6.2,

Carbs 12.1,

Protein 3.7

31. Roasted Mushrooms

Preparation Time: 10 minutes

Cooking Time: 5 minutes

Servings: 2

Ingredients:

- 12 ounces mushroom hats

- ¼ cup fresh dill, chopped

- ¼ teaspoon onion, chopped

- 1 teaspoon olive oil

- ¼ teaspoon turmeric

Directions:

1. Combine the chopped dill and onion.

2. Add the turmeric and stir the mixture.

3. After this, add the olive oil and mix until homogenous.

4. Then fill the mushroom hats with the dill mixture and place them in the air fryer basket.

5. Cook the mushrooms for 5 minutes at 400° F.

6. When the vegetables are cooked, let them cool to room temperature before serving.

Nutrition:

Calories 73,

Fat 3.1,

Fiber 2.6,

Carbs 9.2,

Protein 6.6

32. Mashed Yams

Preparation Time: 10 minutes

Cooking Time: 10 minutes

Servings: 5

Ingredients:

- 1 pound yams

- 1 teaspoon olive oil

- 1 tablespoon almond milk

- ¾ teaspoon salt

- 1 teaspoon dried parsley

Directions:

1. Peel the yams and chop.

2. Place the chopped yams in the air fryer basket and sprinkle with the salt and dried parsley.

3. Add the olive oil and stir the mixture.

4. Cook the yams at 400° F for 10 minutes, stirring twice during cooking.

5. When the yams are done, blend them well with a hand blender until smooth.

6. Add the almond milk and stir carefully.

7. Serve and enjoy!

Nutrition:

Calories 120,

Fat 1.8,

Fiber 3.6,

Carbs 25.1,

Protein 1.4

Chapter 5. Meat

33. Easy Rosemary Lamb Chops

Basic Recipe Preparation Time: 10 minutes

Cooking Time: 6 minutes

Servings: 4

Ingredients:

- 4 lamb chops

- 2 tbsp. dried rosemary

- ¼ cup fresh lemon juice

- Pepper

- Salt

Directions:

1. In a small bowl, mix together lemon juice, rosemary, pepper, and salt. Brush lemon juice rosemary mixture over lamb chops. Place lamb chops on the air fryer oven tray and air fry at 400 F for 3 minutes.

2. Turn lamb chops to the other side and cook for 3 minutes more. Serve and enjoy.

Nutrition: Calories: 267 Fat: 21.7 g Carbs: 1.4 g Protein: 16.9 g

34. BBQ Pork Ribs

Basic Recipe

Preparation Time: 10 minutes

Cooking Time: 12 minutes

Servings: 6

Ingredients:

- 1 slab baby back pork ribs, cut into pieces

- ½ cup BBQ sauce

- ½ tsp paprika

- Salt

Directions:

1. Add pork ribs to a mixing bowl. Add BBQ sauce, paprika, and salt over pork ribs and coat well, and set aside for 30 minutes.

2. Preheat the instant vortex air fryer oven to 350 F. Arrange marinated pork ribs on the instant vortex air fryer oven pan and cook for 10-12 minutes. Turn halfway through.

3. Serve and enjoy.

Nutrition: Calories: 145 Fat: 7 g Carbs: 10 g Protein: 9 g

35. Juicy Steak Bites

Basic Recipe

Preparation Time: 10 minutes

Cooking Time: 9 minutes

Servings: 4

Ingredients:

- 1 lb. sirloin steak, cut into bite-size pieces

- 1 tbsp. steak seasoning

- 1 tbsp. olive oil

- Pepper

- Salt

Directions:

1. Preheat the instant vortex air fryer oven to 390 F.

2. Add steak pieces into the large mixing bowl. Add steak seasoning, oil, pepper, and salt over steak pieces and toss until well coated.

3. Transfer steak pieces on instant vortex air fryer pan and air fry for 5 minutes.

4. Turn steak pieces to the other side and cook for 4 minutes more.

5. Serve and enjoy.

Nutrition:

Calories: 241

Fat: 10.6 g

Carbs: 0 g

Protein: 34.4 g

36. Greek Lamb Chops

Basic Recipe

Preparation Time: 10 minutes

Cooking Time: 10 minutes

Servings: 4

Ingredients:

- 2 lbs. lamb chops

- 2 tsp garlic, minced

- 1 ½ tsp dried oregano

- ¼ cup fresh lemon juice

- ¼ cup olive oil

- ½ tsp pepper

- 1 tsp salt

Directions:

1. Add lamb chops in a mixing bowl. Add remaining ingredients over the lamb chops and coat well.

2. Arrange lamb chops on the air fryer oven tray and cook at 400 F for 5 minutes.

3. Turn lamb chops and cook for 5 minutes more.

4. Serve and enjoy.

Nutrition:

Calories: 538

Fat: 29.4 g

Carbs: 1.3 g

Protein: 64 g

37. Easy Beef Roast

Basic Recipe

Preparation Time: 10 minutes

Cooking Time: 45 minutes

Servings: 6

Ingredients:

- 2 ½ lbs. beef roast

- 2 tbsp. Italian seasoning

Directions:

1. Arrange roast on the rotisserie spite.

2. Rub roast with Italian seasoning, then insert into the instant vortex air fryer oven.

3. Air fry at 350 F for 45 minutes or until the internal temperature of the roast reaches 145 F.

4. Slice and serve.

Nutrition:

Calories: 365 Fat: 13.2 g Carbs: 0.5 g Protein: 57.4 g

Chapter 6. Soup and Stews

38. Mediterranean Bamyeh Okra Tomato Stew

Preparation Time: 5 minutes

Cooking Time: 7 minutes

Servings: 4

Ingredients:

- ¼ cup of water

- 2 tablespoons apple cider vinegar

- 1 cup onions, chopped

- 1 tablespoon minced garlic

- 1 ounce canned tomatoes

- 1 tablespoon vegetable broth

- 1 teaspoon smoked paprika

- ½ teaspoon ground allspice

- 1 teaspoon salt

- 1 1/2 pounds fresh okra

Directions:

1. Place all the ingredients, except for the lemon juice and tomato paste into the air fryer. Put in okra last.

2. Cook on high pressure for 2 minutes, let it rest for 5 minutes.

3. Quick release the pressure.

4. Open the lid carefully and add tomato paste in water and then the lemon juice. Stir gently and serve.

Nutrition:

Calories – 85

Protein – 4 g.

Fat – 5 g.

Carbs – 19 g.

39. Air fryer Minestrone Soup

Preparation Time: 10 minutes

Cooking Time: 35 minutes

Servings: 6

Ingredients:

- 2 tablespoons olive oil

- 3 cloves garlic, minced

- 1 onion, diced

- 2 carrots, peeled and diced

- 2 celery stalks, diced

- 1 ½ teaspoons fresh basil

- 1 teaspoon dried oregano

- ½ teaspoon fennel seed

- 6 cups low-sodium chicken broth

- 28 ounce can tomatoes, diced

- 1 can kidney beans, drained and rinsed

- 1 zucchini, chopped

- 1 Parmesan rind

- 1 bay leaf

- 1 bunch kale, chopped and stems removed

- 2 teaspoons red wine vinegar

- kosher salt and freshly ground black pepper

- ⅓ cup Parmesan, grated

- 2 tablespoons fresh parsley leaves, chopped

Directions:

1. Set air fryer to saute, add olive oil, garlic, onion, carrots, and celery. Cook, occasionally stirring, until tender. Stir in basil, oregano, and fennel seeds for a minute, until fragrant.

2. Pour in the chicken stock, tomatoes, kidney beans, zucchini, parmesan rind, and bay leaf. Select the manual high-pressure setting and set it for 5 minutes.

3. When completed, press quick release to remove all pressure.

4. Stir in the kale for about 2 minutes, then stir in red wine vinegar and season with salt and pepper to taste. Ready to serve.

Nutrition:

Calories – 227 Protein – 14 g. Fat – 7 g. Carbs – 26 g.

40. Air fryer Greek Beef Stew

Preparation Time: 15 minutes

Cooking Time: 40 minutes

Servings: 4

Ingredients:

- 1 ½ pounds stew beef cut into small cubes

- ¼ cup of butter

- 8 small onions

- 8 small potatoes

- 2-3 carrots, sliced

- ¾ cups tomato paste

- 1 teaspoon cinnamon

Directions:

1. Set air fryer to saute mode and cook beef in the butter until browned. This will take about 5 minutes. Then remove.

2. Put the onions in the pot and saute for about 5 minutes.

3. Stop saute mode. Add beef back to the pot and then add carrots, potatoes, tomato paste, and cinnamon. Add 2-3 cups of water.

4. Lock the lid and set the pressure to high and cook for 35 minutes.

5. Allow the steam to release naturally for 10 minutes and then quick release remaining pressure.

6. Ready to serve.

Nutrition:

Calories – 479

Protein – 43 g.

Fat – 20 g.

Carbs – 31 g.

Chapter 7. Snack, Appetizer, Side

41. Shrimp Toast

Basic Recipe

Preparation Time: 12 minutes

Cooking Time: 15 minutes

Servings: 4

Ingredients:

- 3 slices firm white bread

- ⅔ cup finely chopped peeled and deveined raw shrimp

- 1 egg white

- 2 cloves garlic, minced

- 2 tablespoons cornstarch

- ¼ teaspoon ground ginger

- Pinch salt

- Freshly ground black pepper

- 2 tablespoons olive oil

Directions:

1. Cut the crusts from the bread using a sharp knife; crumble the crusts to make bread crumbs. Set aside. In a small bowl, combine the shrimp, egg white, garlic, cornstarch, ginger, salt, and pepper, and mix well.

2. Spread the shrimp mixture evenly on the bread to the edges. With a sharp knife, cut each slice into 4 strips.

3. Mix the bread crumbs with the olive oil and pat onto the shrimp mixture. Place the shrimp toasts in the air fryer basket in a single layer; you may need to cook in batches.

4. Air-frying it for 3 to 6 minutes, until crisp and golden brown.

Nutrition:

Calories 121;

Fat 6g

Carbs 7g

Protein 9g

42. Bacon Tater Tots

Basic Recipe

Preparation Time: 5 minutes

Cooking Time: 17 minutes

Servings: 4

Ingredients:

- 24 frozen tater tots

- 6 slices precooked bacon

- 2 tablespoons maple syrup

- 1 cup shredded Cheddar cheese

Directions:

1. Put the tater tots in the air fryer basket. Air-fry for 10 minutes, shaking the basket halfway through the cooking time.

2. Meanwhile, cut the bacon into 1-inch pieces and shred the cheese.

3. Remove the tater tots from the air fryer basket and put them into a 6-by-6-by-2-inch pan. Top with the bacon and Drizzle with the maple syrup. Air-fry for 5 minutes or until the tots and bacon are crisp.

4. Top with the cheese and air-fry for 2 minutes or until the cheese is melted.

Nutrition:

Calories 374

Fat 22g

Carbs 34g

Protein 13g

43. Hash Brown Burchett

Basic Recipe

Preparation Time: 10 minutes

Cooking Time: 10 minutes

Servings: 4

Ingredients:

- 4 frozen hash brown patties

- 1 tablespoon olive oil

- ⅓ cup chopped cherry tomatoes

- 3 tablespoons diced fresh mozzarella

- 2 tablespoons grated Parmesan cheese

- 1 tablespoon balsamic vinegar

- 1 tablespoon minced fresh basil

Directions:

1. Place the hash brown patties in the air fryer in a single layer. Air-fry for 6 to 8 minutes or until the potatoes are crisp, hot, and golden brown.

2. Meanwhile, combine the olive oil, tomatoes, mozzarella, Parmesan, vinegar, and basil in a small bowl. When the

potatoes are done, carefully remove them from the basket and arrange them on a serving plate. Top with the tomato mixture and serve.

Nutrition:

Calories 123

Fat 6g

Carbs 14g

Protein 5g

44. Waffle Fry Poutine

Basic Recipe

Preparation Time: 10 minutes

Cooking Time: 20 minutes

Servings: 4

Ingredients:

- 2 cups frozen waffle cut fries

- 2 teaspoons olive oil

- 1 red bell pepper, chopped

- 2 green onions, sliced

- 1 cup shredded Swiss cheese

- ½ cup bottled chicken gravy

Directions:

1. Toss the waffle fries with olive oil and place them in the air fryer basket. Air-fry for 10 to 12 minutes or until the fries are crisp and light golden brown, shaking the basket halfway through the cooking time.

2. Transfer the fries to a 6-by-6-by-2-inch pan and top with the pepper, green onions, and cheese. Air-fry for 3 minutes until the vegetables are crisp and tender.

3. Remove the pan from the air fryer and Drizzle with the gravy over the fries. Air-fry for 2 minutes or until the gravy is hot. Serve immediately.

Nutrition:

Calories 347;

Fat 19g

Carbs 33g

Protein 12g

45. Crispy Beef Cubes

Basic Recipe

Preparation Time: 10 minutes **Cooking Time:** 20 minutes

Servings: 4

Ingredients:

- 1-pound sirloin tip, cut into 1-inch cubes

- 1 cup cheese pasta sauce (from a 16-ounce jar)

- 1½ cups soft bread crumbs

- 2 tablespoons olive oil

- ½ teaspoon dried marjoram

Directions:

1. In a medium bowl, toss the beef with the pasta sauce to coat.In a shallow bowl, combine the bread crumbs, oil, and marjoram, and mix well. Drop the beef cubes, one at a time, into the bread crumb mixture to coat thoroughly.

2. Cook the beef in two batches for 6 to 8 minutes, shaking the basket once during the cooking time until the beef is at least 145°F and the outside is crisp and brown. Serve with toothpicks or little forks.

Nutrition: Calories 554 Fat 22g Carbs 43g Protein 44g

46. Stuffing hushpuppies

Basic Recipe

Preparation Time: 10 minutes

Cooking Time: 12 minutes

Servings: 3

Ingredients:

- Cooking trays

- 3 cups of cold stuffing

- 1 large egg

Directions:

1. Place the egg in a large bowl and beat it. Add 3 cups of stuffing and stir until they are well combined.

2. Preheat your instant air fryer to 375 degrees Fahrenheit and set it to 12 minutes.

3. Remove the cooking tray and spray it with a cooking spray before adding the hushpuppies into the racks. Spray on top of the hushpuppies as well. Cook for 6 minutes before flipping.

4. Once you are halfway, flip the hushpuppies to allow for the other side to cook well. Repeat this with the remaining hush puppies.

5. Serve with a sauce of your choice.

Nutrition:

Calories 237.4

Fat 16.6g

Carbs 18.8g

Proteins 3.2g

47. Fried Green Tomatoes

Basic Recipe

Preparation Time: 10 minutes

Cooking Time: 15 minutes

Servings: 6

Ingredients:

- 1 cup bread crumbs

- 1/3 cup of versatile flour

- 1 cup yellow cornmeal

- 2 tomatoes cut into little slices

- ½ cup buttermilk

- 2 eggs, beaten gently

Directions:

1. Season the slices of tomato with pepper and salt. Take 3 breeding meals.

2. Keep flour in the very first, stir in eggs and buttermilk in the 2nd, and mix cornmeal and bread crumbs in the third.

3. Dig up the pieces of tomato in your flour, shaking off any excess.

4. Now dip the tomatoes in the egg mix, then in the bread crumb mixture to coat both sides.

5. Preheat your air fryer to 400 degrees F. Brush olive oil on the fryer basket.

6. Keep the pieces of tomato in your fryer basket.

7. Brush some olive oil on the tomato tops, cook for 10 minutes, flip your tomatoes, brush olive oil and cook for another 5 minutes. Take the tomatoes out.

8. Keep in a rack lined with a paper towel. Serve.

Nutrition:

Calories 246

Carbs 40g

Fat 6g

Chapter 8. Desserts

48. Walnut Apple Pear Mix

Preparation Time: 10 minutes

Cooking Time: 10 minutes

Servings: 4

Ingredients:

- 2 apples, cored and cut into wedges

- 1/2 tsp vanilla

- 1 cup apple juice

- 2 tbsp. walnuts, chopped

- 2 apples, cored and cut into wedges

Directions:

1. Put all of the ingredients in the inner pot of the air fryer and stir well. Seal pot and cook on high for 10 minutes.

2. As soon as the cooking is done, let it release pressure naturally for 10 minutes, then release remaining using quick release. Remove lid. Serve and enjoy.

Nutrition: Calories – 132 Protein – 1.3 g. Fat – 2.6 g. Carbs – 28.3 g

49. Cinnamon Pear Jam

Preparation Time: 10 minutes

Cooking Time: 4 minutes

Servings: 12

Ingredients:

- 8 pears, cored and cut into quarters

- 1 tsp cinnamon

- 1/4 cup apple juice

- 2 apples, peeled, cored, and diced

Directions:

1. Put all of the ingredients in the inner pot of the air fryer and stir well.

2. Seal pot and cook on high for 4 minutes.

3. As soon as the cooking is done, let it release pressure naturally. Remove lid.

4. Blend pear apple mixture using an immersion blender until smooth. Serve and enjoy.

Nutrition: Calories – 103 Protein – 0.6 g.Fat – 0.3 g. Carbs – 27.1 g.

50. Cinnamon Pudding

Preparation Time: 5 minutes

Cooking Time: 12 minutes

Servings: 2

Ingredients:

- 4 eggs; whisked

- 4 tbsp. erythritol

- 2 tbsp. heavy cream

- ½ tsp. cinnamon powder

- ¼ tsp. allspice, ground

- Cooking spray

Directions:

1. Take a bowl and mix all the ingredients, except the cooking spray, whisk well and pour into a ramekin greased with cooking spray.

2. Add the basket to your Air Fryer, put the ramekin inside, and cook at 400°F for 12 minutes. Divide into bowls and serve for breakfast.

Nutrition: Calories: 201 Fat: 11g Fiber: 2g Carbs: 4g Protein: 6g

51. Carrot Mug Cake

Preparation Time: 15 minutes

Cooking Time: 20 minutes

Serving: 1

Ingredients:

- ¼ cup whole-wheat pastry flour

- 1 tablespoon coconut sugar

- ¼ teaspoon baking powder

- 1/8 teaspoon ground cinnamon

- 1/8 teaspoon ground ginger

- Pinch of ground cloves

- Pinch of ground allspice

- Pinch of salt

- 2 tablespoons plus 2 teaspoons unsweetened almond milk

- 2 tablespoons carrot, peeled and grated

- 2 tablespoons walnuts, chopped

- 1 tablespoon raisins

- 2 teaspoons applesauce

Directions:

1. In a bowl, mix together the flour, sugar, baking powder, spices and salt.

2. Add the remaining ingredients and mix until well combined.

3. Place the mixture into a lightly greased ramekin.

4. Press "Power Button" of Air Fry Oven and turn the dial to select the "Air Bake" mode.

5. Press the Time button and again turn the dial to set the cooking time to 20 minutes.

6. Now push the Temp button and rotate the dial to set the temperature at 350 degrees F.

7. Press "Start/Pause" button to start.

8. When the unit beeps to show that it is preheated, open the lid.

9. Arrange the ramekin over the "Wire Rack" and insert in the oven. Place the ramekin onto a wire rack to cool slightly before serving.

Nutrition: Calories 301 Fat 10.1 g Carbs: 14g Protein 7.6 g

Conclusion

Now that you reached the end of this book, those recipes will give you different vibes and make you feel like an expert chef by using your Instant Vortex Air Fryer. Try the recipes in this book and give yourself and your family something to look forward to even on weekdays.

Air Fry: using this program to cook oil-free, crispy food, whether it's coated meat or fries, everything can be fried in its Air fryer basket.

Toast: the temp/time dial used to set the temperature and cooking time can be used to select the bread slices and their brownness when they need to be toasted using the Toast cooking program of the Instant Air Fryer toaster oven.

Bake: it is used to bake cakes, brownies, or bread in a quick time.

Broil: the broiler's settings provide direct top-down heat to crisp meat, melt cheese, and caramelizes the vegetables and fruits. It has the default highest temperature, which is 450 degrees F.

Dehydrate: low-temperature heat is regulated to effectively remove moisture from foods, thus giving perfect crispy veggie chips, jerky, and dehydrated fruits.

For a longer usage or its span, always remember that the Instant Air Fryer Toaster Oven must be cleaned after every cooking session like any other cooking appliance. It is important to keep the inside of the oven germs free all the time. The food particles that are stuck at the base or on the oven's walls should be cleaned after every session using the following steps:

Unplug the Instant Air Fryer toaster oven and allow it to cool down completely. Keep the door open while it cools down. Remove all the trays, dripping pan, steel racks, and other accessories from inside the oven.

Place the removable parts of the oven in the dishwasher and wash them thoroughly. Once these accessories are washed, all of them dry out completely. Meanwhile, take a clean and slightly damp cloth to clean the inside of the oven.